500
WaYS To MaKE Me
LAUGH
UNTiL I

Cry!

500
WAYS TO MAKE ME

LAUGH
UNTIL I
Cry!

Ticktock

An Hachette UK Company

www.hachette.co.uk

First published in Great Britain in 2014 by Ticktock,
an imprint of Octopus Publishing Group Ltd
Endeavour House
189 Shaftesbury Avenue
London
WC2H 8JY

www.octopusbooks.co.uk
www.ticktockbooks.co.uk

ISBN 978 1 78325 088 2

A CIP record for this book is available from the British Library.

Printed and bound in the UK by CPI Group (UK) Ltd, Croydon, CR0 4YY

10 9 8 7 6 5 4 3 2 1

Text, illustration and design: Duck Egg Blue
Project Editor: Mariangela Palazzi-Williams
Publisher: Samantha Sweeney
Managing Editor: Karen Rigden
Production Controller: Sarah Connelly

THE END

Contents

Too Cool for School

Mum: Time to get up and go to school!

Son: I don't want to go. Everyone hates me and I get bullied!

Mum: But you have to go. You're the head teacher!

Why did the student throw his watch out of the school window?

He wanted to see time fly!

Mum: From now on you are going to have free school dinners.

Son: But Mum, I don't want three school dinners. One is more than enough!

RIDDLE

How do you make the number one disappear?

Add the letter G and it's 'GONE'!

John: Great news! The teacher said we're going to have a test today, come rain or shine.

Sam: So what's so great about that?

John: It's snowing!

Dinner Lady: It's very rude to reach over the table for cakes. Haven't you got a tongue?

Pupil: Yes, but my arms are longer!

What do get when you cross one head teacher with another?

I wouldn't do it - head teachers don't like to be crossed!

Why did the teacher go to the beach?

He wanted to test the water!

What's a teacher's favourite nation?

Expla-nation!

Why did the teacher wear sunglasses?

Because her class was so bright!

Teacher: Holly, why didn't you go straight home from school?

Holly: Because I live around the corner!

Why did the clock go to the head teacher's office?

It was tocking too much!

Why did the new boy steal a chair from the classroom?

Because the teacher told him to take a seat!

Why were the teacher's eyes crossed?

Because she couldn't control her pupils!

Why did the jelly bean go to school?

To become a smartie!

"My father gave me a really cheap dictionary for my birthday, but I couldn't find the words to thank him!"

Which hand is it better to write with?

Neither, you should use a pen!

Daughter: Dad, can you write in the dark?

Dad: I can have a go. What do you want me to write?

Daughter: Your signature on my report!

Why have nursery teachers got such a positive attitude?

They know how to make the little things count!

Teacher: I think you need glasses, Lewis.

Lewis: What makes you think that, Mr Johnson?

Teacher: You're facing the wrong way!

Why does your teacher have her hair in a bun?

Because she has her nose in a burger!

Teacher: Emma, I wish you'd pay a little attention.

Emma: I'm paying as little as I can!

Teacher: Did your mum or dad help you with the questions?

Ryan: No, I got them wrong all by myself!

Teacher: Why did you bring eye shadow and lipstick to school, Eva? You know it is forbidden!

Eva: But miss, you told me I had to do a make-up test today because of the low mark I got yesterday!

Teacher: Which two words in English have the most letters?

Erin: Post Office!

13

What happened to the plant when it went to its maths lesson?

It grew square roots!

Dad: Holly, why is your test score so low?

Holly: Because of absence

Dad: You were absent?

Holly: No, but the girl next to me was!

If a picture is worth a thousand words, then why shouldn't we judge a book by its cover?

What's a mushroom?

The place they store the school food!

Teacher: Did you know that most accidents happen in the kitchen?

Freddie: Yes, but we still have to eat them!

Why did the school canteen hire a dentist?

To make more filling meals!

Why was the broom late for school?

It overswept!

Teacher: Who invented King Arthur's round table?

Pupil: Was it Sir Cumference?

Is the new teacher strict?

I don't know. I'm too scared to ask!

I usually wear a bright coat, have a black tip and make marks wherever I go. What am I?

A pencil!

I would tell you a joke about this blunt pencil, but it would be pointless.

Left shelf

Slow Cooking!
by Stu Pot

Hidden Treasures in the Loft
by Anne Teak

THE TWELFTH MONTH
by Dee Sember

Magic Words
by Abi Cadabra.

The Nervous Skydiver
by Hugo First

Good Luck!
by Bess Twishes

Right shelf

HOW TO BUILD A ROBOT
by Anne Droid

Red vegetables
by B. Troot

Just Say No!
by Will Power

How to Treat Insect Bites
by Ivor Nitch

Housework
by Dustin Cook

Ghost, Ghouls and Goblins
by Emma Fraid

What did the pencil say to the protractor?

"Take me to your ruler!"

Teacher: Why are you doing your multiplications on the floor?

Max: You told me not to use tables!

Why did the teacher turn the lights on?

Because her class was so dim.

What's an inkling?

A baby fountain pen!

Why did Henry VIII have so many wives?

He liked to chop and change!

Jess: Is the maths teacher in a good mood today?

Freya: I wouldn't count on it!

Geography teacher: John, where is Turkey?

John: I have no idea, sir. I haven't seen it since Christmas!

I've always had a hard time with decimals - I just can't see the point!

Teacher: Ian, if you had 50p in one pocket and 70p in the other pocket, what would you have?

Ian: Somebody else's trousers, Miss.

END OF YEAR SCHOOL REPORT

Pupil: Bridget D. Fidget

Subject: Maths

With grades like these, at least we know she doesn't cheat.

Subject: English

The improvement in Bridget's handwriting has revealed that she can't spell.

Subject: PE

Bridget has great speed, it's just a shame she runs in the wrong direction.

Subject: Music

I can only assume Bridget has an excellent ear for music as she's always listening to her mp3 player.

Subject: Geography

Bridget does well to find the classroom.

If teachers are so smart, how come their books are the ones with the answers in?

Geography teacher: Where's the Dead Sea?

Ewan: Dead? I never knew it was sick!

Geography teacher: Why did the explorers go to the South Pole?

Grace: To visit Aunt Arctica.

What happened when the wheel was invented?

It caused a revolution!

21

Knock, knock,
who's there?
Norway
Norway who?
Norway am I telling
you any more
knock, knock jokes!

Who invented fire?

Some bright spark!

Why does history keep repeating itself?

Because nobody was listening the first time around!

"Ben, were the pyramids built by the Ancient Egyptians?"

"I sphinx so sir!"

What kind of lunches do geometry teachers enjoy?

Square meals!

Did you hear about the maths teacher whose mistakes started to multiply?

In the end, they had to take him away!

When I grow up I want to be a...

POLICE OFFICER
Hans Cuffs

PLUMBER
Lee King

PRIVATE DETECTIVE
Ivor Clue

DENTIST
Phil McCavity

GEOLOGIST
Roxanne Minerals

ACCOUNTANT
Penny Pincher

LUMBERJACK
Tim Burr

LONG-DISTANCE LORRY DRIVER
Miles Apart

FORTUNE TELLER
Claire Voyance

Sporting Shenanigans

Knock Knock!
Who's there?
General Lee
General Lee who?
Generally I go to training, but today I've got a match!

How did the football pitch become a triangle?

Somebody took a corner!

Why is a doughnut like a golfer?

It has a hole in one!

What can you serve, but not eat?

A tennis ball!

Why are football stadiums odd?

Because you sit in the stands, but you can't stand in the seats!

Why weren't the basketball players invited for dinner?

Because they dribbled too much!

Referee: William, I'm sending you off the football pitch!

William: What for?

Referee: The rest of the match!

What's the quietest sport?

Bowling – you can hear a pin drop!

What do you call a cat that plays football?

Puss in boots!

What do you call a very clever tennis player?

A racket scientist!

What goes putt-putt-putt-putt?

A dreadful golfer!

Why can't waiters play tennis?

They only want to serve!

Knock Knock!
Who's there?
Caddy.
Caddy who?
Caddy your own clubs, mate!

How many golfers does it take to change a light bulb?

Fore!

PLEASE DON'T PICK UP LOST BALLS UNTIL THEY STOP ROLLING!

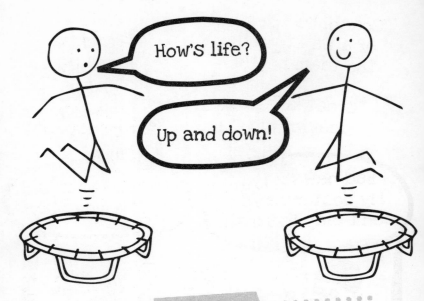

RIDDLE

What do you throw out when you want to use it, but take in when you don't want to use it?

A fishing line!

What musical instruments do Spanish fishermen play?

Cast-a-nets!

Why is a football stadium always cold?

Because it's full of fans!

"Coach, I've thought of a way to make the team better."

"Great, are you leaving it?"

Why did the basketball player go to the doctor?

To get more shots!

Bad news guys. My doctor says I can't play baseball.

Really? When did he see you play?

RIDDLE

What is harder to catch the further you run?

Your breath!

Where do old bowling balls end up?

The gutter!

What is a goalkeeper's favourite snack?

Cheese on post!

Which part of a swimming pool is never the same?

The changing rooms!

What kind of cats go bowling?

Alley cats!

Don't stop me. I'm on a roll!

Knock Knock!
Who's there?
Canoe.
Canoe who?
Canoe come out and play today?

What is a cheerleader's favourite colour?

Yeller!

CRACKING PANTS!

You will need: A piece of cloth and a water fountain.

Take a piece of old cloth with you to football or rugby training, making sure you keep it well hidden.

Follow your victim when they go to the water fountain. As they bend over to drink, tear the cloth to make a ripping sound.

Thinking that their trousers have ripped, your victim will race back to the changing room, while you just watch and laugh!

PRANK LIKE A PRO: Select the right cloth and try out the ripping noise at home first – a piece of old cotton sheet is perfect.

Look! The target is making an arrow escape!

What happened when two balls of string had a race?

They ended up in a tie!

Two riders on a tandem bicycle reach the top of a mountain, puffing and panting. "Phew, that was a hard climb," said the rider at the back. "You're not kidding," replied the rider at the front. "It's a good job I kept the brakes on, or we would have slid back down the hill!"

All Creatures Great and Small

What does an oyster do on her birthday?

She shellebrates!

Where do sheep go to get their hair cut?

The baa baas!

What's the most musical fish?

The piano tuna!

How do toads greet one another?

"Wart's up?"

What did the snake say to his girlfriend after they had an argument?

"Let's hiss and make up!"

What kind of animal goes 'oom'?

A cow walking backwards!

Where do turtles go when it rains?

To shell-ter!

What do birds watch on the TV?

The feather forecast!

When does a cow get a bunch of flowers and breakfast in bed?

On M-udders Day!

How do rabbits keep their fur tidy?

With hare-spray!

What do you call a young goat that practises martial arts?

The Karate Kid!

Why didn't the mussel have any friends?

Because he was a little shellfish!

What do cows play at birthday parties?

Moosical chairs!

Why did the tadpole feel lonely?

Because he was newt to the area!

What do you get when you cross a cow with a camel?

Lumpy milkshakes!

What's a skunk's favourite game in school?

Show and smell!

What do you call a sleeping bull?

A bulldozer!

What do you get when you cross an angry sheep with an angry cow?

An animal in a very baaaaaad moooood!

What did the forgetful skunk say when the wind changed direction?

"It's all coming back to me now!"

Why was the little bear so spoiled?

Because its mother panda'd to its every whim!

Where do penguins vote?

At the South Poll!

Why did the skunk buy four boxes of tissues?

Because he had a stinking cold!

A snail entered a police station and told an officer, 'I've just been mugged by two turtles. They beat me up and took all my money!" The officer replied, "Why that's terrible. Did you get a good look at them?" "No sir, it all happened so fast!"

What's a skunk's philosophy of life?

Eat, stink and be merry!

What did one slug say to the other?

"Slime flies when you're having fun!"

What did the farmer get when he crossed a centipede with a turkey?

100 drumsticks!

What happened to the leopard who took a bath three times a day?

After a week he was spotless!

A man looks out his window and sees a snail on his best plant. He goes outside, picks up the snail and throws him as far as he can. Two years later the man hears a tap, tap, tap on his window. To his amazement he sees the same snail, who looks right at him and asks "What did you do that for?"

What did the hungry dalmatian say after his dinner?

"That hit the spots!"

Why can't dalmatians play hide and seek?

They are always spotted!

A WILD ENCOUNTER!

You will need: A phone and the phone number of a local zoo or wildlife park.

Make a note of the phone number for the local zoo. Call your house number from your mobile phone when your mum is busy and pretend to answer it.

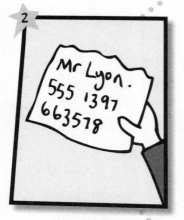

Tell your mum that someone called Mr Lyon was on the phone and he asked if she could call him back. Give her the number of the zoo and have a good giggle when she phones them up asking to be put through to the king of the jungle!

PRANK LIKE A PRO: Make sure you pronounce 'Lyon' as the animal or the joke won't work.

What did the duck say when she bought some lipstick?

"Put it on my bill!"

What do you call a pig that does karate?

A pork chop!

RIDDLE

You are on a horse, galloping at a constant speed. You are surrounded by animals, all running in the same direction as you. Just behind you there is a huge lion which is running at the same speed as you. What can you do to escape this dangerous situation?

Get off the merry-go-round!

What do you get if you cross a chicken with a cement mixer?

A bricklayer!

Where do you buy baby birds?

At the chickout!

What is the quietest kind of dog?

A hush puppy!

Why did the duck cross the road?

To prove he wasn't a chicken!

What do whales eat?

Fish and ships!

What bird is with you at every meal?

A swallow!

What do you call a bird in the winter?

Brrr-d!

Boy: I'd like to buy some bird seed.

Shop Assistant: OK. How many birds do you have?

Boy: None! I want to grow some!

Knock Knock!
Who's there?
Kook!
Kook who?
Don't call me cuckoo!

A man was driving down the road with three penguins in his car. A policeman asked him to pull over. "Why have you got three penguins in your car? You must take them to the zoo," he said. The next day the policeman saw the man again. He still had the penguins in the back of his car. "Hey, I thought I told you yesterday to take those penguins to the zoo," said the officer. "I did," said the man, "and they loved it! Today I'm taking them to the beach!"

There were two cows in a field. The first cow said "moo" and the second cow said "baaaa". "Why did you say baaaa?" the first cow asked the second cow. "I'm learning a foreign language," the second cow replied.

What should you do if your dog chews a dictionary?

Take the words out of his mouth!

How does a mouse feel after it takes a shower?

Squeaky clean!

What did one firefly say to the other?

"I've got to glow now!"

What do you call 100 spiders on a tyre?

A spinning wheel!

Why was the baby ant confused?

Because all his uncles were ants!

What do you call a thieving alligator?

A crookodile!

What do you get if you cross a firefly and a moth?

An insect that can see its way around a dark wardrobe!

What do you call a fly without wings?

A walk!

Who is a bee's favourite painter?

Pablo Beecasso!

What has antlers and sucks blood?

A moose-quito!

Why was the ladybird kicked out of the forest?

Because she was a litter bug!

Why did the spider take her laptop to the beach?

So she could surf the web!

What do you get if you cross a centipede and a parrot?

A walkie-talkie!

50

Why don't centipedes play football?

It takes too long to put their boots on!

Why did the firefly keep stealing things?

He was light-fingered!

What did one girl firefly say to the other?

You glow girl!

What's a spider's favourite meal?

Corn on the cobweb!

Who is a bee's favourite singer?

Sting!

What is both on the ground and a hundred feet in the air?

A centipede on its back!

What do moths study in school?

Mothematics!

Did you hear about the caterpillars that got married?

It was larva at first sight!

What do you call a bug that can't have too much sugar?

A diabeetle!

What does a spider do when he gets angry?

He goes up the wall!

What kind of petrol do snails buy?

Shell!

He's so cute. You must be so proud!

What do you call two spiders that just got married?

Newly webs!

What lives in gum trees?

Stick insects!

When do spiders go on their honeymoon?

After their webbing day!

What's black, yellow and covered in blackberries?

A bramble bee!

What kind of bugs live in clocks?

Ticks!

What do fireflies eat?

Light snacks!

ICE COOL BUGS!

You will need: Small fake bugs from a joke or toy shop and an ice cube tray.

Place a fake bug in each compartment of the ice tray. Fill the ice tray with water and freeze.

When someone asks for ice, pop the bug-filled ice cubes in their glass and watch as they freak out!

PRANK LIKE A PRO: Choose the right moment for maximum effect. A party or a family celebration is the perfect occasion to share a nice practical joke and have a laugh together!

What did one bee say to the other bee on a sunny day?

"Swarm today, isn't it?"

Who is a bee's favourite pop group?

The bee gees!

What's a bee-line?

The shortest distance between two buzz-stops!

Funny Folk

What do you call the child of parents from Iceland and Cuba?

An ice cube!

Girl, talking to her brother: "I didn't recognise you for a moment. It was one of the happiest moments in my life!"

Hey, little sis, why did you tell everyone at school I am an idiot?

Sorry, I didn't know it was a secret!

"Dad, does money grow on trees?"

"Of course not, darling."

"Then why do banks have branches?"

How do you know that carrots are good for your eyesight?

Have you ever seen a rabbit wearing glasses?

Little Susie complained, "Mum, my tummy aches." "That's because your tummy is empty," her mother replied. "You would feel better if you had something in it." That evening her father complained that he had a headache. "That's because it's empty," Susie said. "You'd feel better if you had something in it!"

"What's your father's occupation?" asked the teacher on the first day of school. "He's a magician, Miss," answered the new boy. "He saws people in half." "Gosh!" replied the teacher. "Do you have any brothers or sisters?" "One half brother and two half sisters!"

I've got a good idea!

Must be beginner's luck!

Bobby: Katie, why are you taking that pencil to bed?

Katie: To draw the curtains, silly!

CRAZY TIME TURNER!

You will need: As many watches, alarm clocks and clocks as you can find.

When nobody is looking, change the time forward by at least an hour on all the clocks in the house. Keep your watch unchanged, so that you know what the actual time is.

We're late!

Watch your victims run around like headless chickens trying to work out the time while getting ready for their meeting. Keep a safe distance... they will be very annoyed!

PRANK LIKE A PRO: Don't be cruel. Give them plenty of time to get to their appointment!

I've changed my mind.

Finally! Does the new one work any better?

What's the best present ever?

A broken drum. You can't beat that!

Mother: Are you talking back to me?

Son: Well yeah, that's how communication works.

What did the speak-your-weight machine say when Auntie Maureen stepped on it?

"One at a time, please!"

A mother takes her son to buy a pair of school shoes. As he tries them on, the shop assistant asks "How do they feel?" "The right one feels a bit tight", the boy replies. "Oh, but you have to try it with the tongue out!" The boy looks at her and replies "Thorry, it thill feelth a bit thight!"

Mum's cooking is improving! The smoke isn't as black as it used to be!

What's a baby's motto?

If at first you don't succeed, cry, cry and cry again!

A ZESTY DRINK!

You will need: Two plastic bottles, water and some clear vinegar.

Fill a couple of plastic water bottles with water. Add a few drops of vinegar to one of them and then pop them both in the fridge. Convince your victim to go for a jog or a long bike ride and take the bottles with you.

Here, have a drink!

When you stop for a break, start drinking from your bottle. Offer the other one to your victim, then take cover as they spit it back out again!

PRANK LIKE A PRO: Use bottles with different colour tops to make sure you don't get them mixed up. And carry an extra bottle of clean water for your victim: they'll need it!

Dad: John, would you like a pocket calculator for Christmas?

Son: No, dad. I already know how many pockets I have, thanks!

Mother: William, you've put your shoes on the wrong feet!

William: But these are the only feet I've got!

RIDDLE

Mark's mum has four children. The first is called April, the second is called May and the third is called June. What's the fourth called?

Mark!

What happened to the granny that put her false teeth in backwards?

She ate herself!

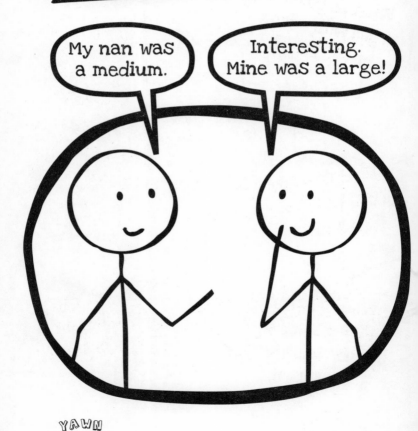

What do you call...

What do you call a girl across a river?

Bridget!

What do you call a girl with a frog on her head?

Lily!

What do you call a girl with a cash register on her head?

Tilly!

What do you call a boy with a spade on his head?

Doug!

What do you call a boy on your doorstep?

Matt!

67

A guard asked a prisoner what he was in jail for. "Doing my Christmas shopping early," replied the man. "That doesn't seem a crime to me!" replied the officer. "It is if the shops haven't opened yet!"

Why are pirate flags always in a bad mood?

Because they have crossbones!

What do you call an underwater spy?

James Pond!

What did the pirate name his daughter?

Peggy!

YAW

One day a postman was greeted by a boy and a huge dog. The mailman asked the boy, "Does your dog bite?" "No," replied the boy. Just then the dog bit the postman. The man yelled, "I thought you said your dog doesn't bite!" "I did" replied the boy. "But that's not my dog!"

Postman 1: A dog bit me on the leg this morning.

Postman 2: Did you put anything on it?

Postman 1: No, he liked it plain.

Why does it take pirates so long to learn the alphabet?

Because they spend years at C!

How much did the pirate pay for his hook and peg leg?

An arm and a leg!

What do you get if you cross a painter with a policeman?

A brush with the law!

A police recruit was asked during the exam, "What would you do if you had to arrest your own mother?"

He said, "Call for backup."

What are two robbers called?

A pair of nickers!

What did the lawyer name his daughter?

Sue!

Why did the book join the police?

It wanted to go undercover!

Why did the tap dancer retire?

He kept falling into the sink!

An armed robber went into a bank and shouted "Gimme all your money or you're geography!" "Er," said the stunned cashier, "don't you mean history?" "Shut up," shouted the robber. "And don't change the subject!"

What happened to the robber who pinched a bar of soap?

He made a clean getaway!

Did you hear about the identical twins who robbed a bank?

After they were caught, they finished each other's sentences!

How did the grave digger get his job?

He just fell into it!

Did you hear about the man who bought a paper shop?

It blew away!

What is an archaeologist?

Someone whose career is in ruins!

Did you hear about the two little boys who found themselves in a modern art gallery? "Quick," said one, "Run! Before they say we did it!"

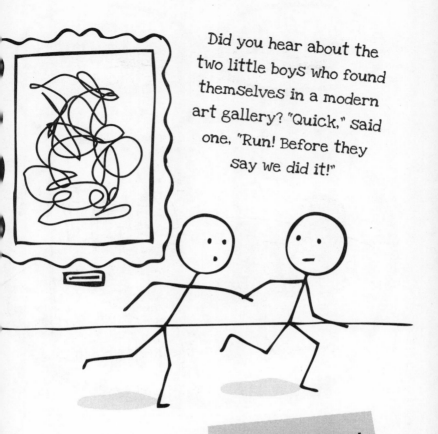

Why did the handyman have to get false teeth?

He kept biting his nails!

Did you hear about the florist who had two sons?

One is a budding genius and the other is a blooming idiot!

Why did the clown wear loud socks?

So his feet wouldn't fall asleep!

What kind of training do you need to be a rubbish collector?

None - you just pick it up as you go along!

Daft Dinners

Why did the biscuit cry?

Because its mum had been a wafer so long!

Why did the carrot look down the toilet?

He wondered where the peas had gone!

You use a knife to slice my head and weep beside me when I am dead. What am I?

An onion!

What are the worst vegetables to serve on a boat?

Leeks!

Customer: Excuse me, waiter. Will my pizza be long?

Waiter: Er, no sir, it'll be round!

How do you make an onion giggle?

Pickle it!

How do you fix a broken pizza?

With tomato paste!

You throw away the outside and cook the inside. Then you eat the outside and throw away the inside. What is it?

An ear of corn!

Did you hear about the strawberry who attended charm school?

He became a real smoothie!

What's the opposite of a somersault?

A winter pepper!

JELLIED JUICE!

You will need: Plastic cups, straws and some raspberry jelly cubes.

Dissolve the jelly cubes in warm water, following the instructions on the packet.

Place a straw in each plastic cup and pour in the jelly while it's still liquid. Place in the fridge for a few hours to set.

Once set, place the cups on the table and invite your friends to take a drink. Now watch them and giggle as they struggle to take a sip!

PRANK LIKE A PRO: Prepare a normal raspberry drink for yourself and start drinking it before everybody else. Make sure you hold down the straw so that they don't notice the difference with their drink.

What did one strawberry say to the other?

"Look at the jam you've got us into!"

Why are chefs mean?

They beat eggs, whip cream and mash potatoes!

What do you call an overweight pumpkin?

Plumpkin!

Why did the apple go out with a fig?

It couldn't find a date!

Did you hear about the apple crumble, rhubarb crumble and gooseberry crumble trial?

They all ended up in custardy!

What do you get if you cross a Shakespeare play with an egg?

Omelette!

Danny, how many times do I have to tell you to keep away from that jar of biscuits?

No more times. It's empty!

How do you start a jelly race?

Get set!

Knock Knock!

Who's there?

Figs.

Figs who?

Figs the doorbell, it's broken!

What do you call a lazy baker?

A loafer!

81

"Waiter, is there soup on the menu?"

"No, sir. I wiped it off!"

"Waiter, do you serve crabs?"

"Of course, sir. We serve anybody!"

What did one plate say to the other plate?

"Lunch is on me!"

Why was the chef so relaxed?

He had plenty of thyme on his hands!

What animal is like a yoghurt?

A moose!

What did the nut say when it sneezed?

"A cashew!"

"Waiter, can I have my lunch on the patio?"

"Certainly Sir, but most people prefer to have it on the plate!"

I thought you were on a Seafood diet?

I am. When I see food, I eat it!

84

Why couldn't the teddy bear eat his food?

Because he was stuffed!

"I got food poisoning from dinosaur meat the other day. I ate it ROAR!"

What did the mayonnaise say when someone opened the refrigerator door?

"Close the door, I'm dressing!"

What's the best thing to put into a pie?

Your teeth!

What do rubbish collectors eat?

Junk food!

Knock Knock!
Who's there?
Justin!
Justin who?
Justin time
for lunch!

What do snowmen like to eat for breakfast?

Frosted flakes!

I always talk to my food before I eat. It's the only way I can be sure it will agree with me.

Why couldn't the Christmas turkey escape the roasting pan?

He was foiled!

FROZEN BREAKFAST!

You will need: A bowl, milk, cereal and a freezer.

Pour some milk in the bowl and add your victim's favourite cereal.

Place the bowl of milk and cereal in the freezer and leave it overnight.

The next morning, offer to prepare breakfast. Place the frozen cereal and a spoon in front of your victim and watch them as they try to eat their breakfast!

PRANK LIKE A PRO: To make your serving more realistic, top it up at the last minute with some fresh milk and a sprinkle of cereal.

87

It's a Crazy World

What did the envelope say to the stamp?

"Stick with me and we'll go places!"

What do penguins do on holiday?

Chill!

Where do pianists go on holiday?

The Florida Keys!

Why did the dalmatian take so long to choose his holiday?

He was looking for the right spot!

What do you call a man-made holiday island?

Con-Crete!

Where do cows go on holiday?

Moo York!

A businessman was struggling to carry his lumpy, oversized bag onto the plane. Helped by a flight attendant, he finally managed to stuff it into the overhead compartment. "Do you always carry such heavy luggage?" she sighed. "This is the last time" the man said. "Next time, I'm going in the bag and my wife can buy the ticket!"

Sorry, I couldn't book our holiday because the sign in the window at the travel agent said 'GO AWAY!'

What do you call a passenger covered in salt and pepper?

A seasoned traveller!

My luggage wasn't on the belt, so I would like to report that it's lost.

Has your plane arrived yet?

AIRPORT LOST LUGGAGE

A Scotsman visiting London was checking out of his hotel. "And how was your stay, sir?" asked the receptionist as he paid the bill. "Terrible!" he said. "At four o'clock this morning there was so much banging. Banging on the walls, banging on the door - even banging on the ceiling. It was so loud I could hardly hear myself playing the bagpipes!"

HIDDEN SURPRISE!

You will need: A beach towel and a spade.

While at the beach, convince your victim to go and get an ice cream. When they're out of sight, remove their beach towel and start digging a hole in the sand, then remove all evidence of the sand you've dug up.

Replace the towel making sure it covers the hole and is flat on the ground. Then wait for your victim to return and invite him or her to sit down and enjoy their ice cream!

PRANK LIKE A PRO: Don't make the hole too deep or too wide – a little dent in the sand is enough for them to sink in!

A guide is showing a group of tourists around a castle. "Nothing has changed – not a stone has been touched in over 500 years," he explained. "Really?" said one of the tourists. "We must have the same landlord!"

What do you get when you throw a million books into the ocean?

A title wave!

A young man turns up at a hotel reception. "I'd like a single room, please," he asks. "Certainly, sir," says the receptionist. "With bath or shower?" The man doesn't have much money, so he asks, "What's the difference?" "You have to stand in the shower," replies the receptionist.

H

What do you call six weeks of rain in Scotland?

Summer!

What's the biggest problem with snow boots?

They melt!

What did one Arctic explorer say to the other Arctic explorer?

"I'd hate to have a bear behind in this weather!"

How do you dress in Sweden during winter?

Quickly!

What is the fastest country in the world?

Russia!

Why is Britain the wettest country?

Because royalty has reigned there for years!

SHORT SHEETS!

You will need: A bed made with sheets and blankets.

Take all the bedding off the bed, leaving the bottom sheet on the mattress.

Lay the top sheet on the bed, so that the end that is usually at the pillow end is at the bottom. If there's a pattern on the sheet, make sure it's facing down.

Tuck the top sheet under the mattress at the pillow end and fold the sheet in half so that the bottom edge is now at the pillow end, too.

Replace the blanket and fold the top edge of the sheet over it. Tuck in the edges and return the pillow to the bed. When your victim goes to bed, they'll find that they can't lie down properly!

PRANK LIKE A PRO: Cover your tracks by making sure the bed is neatly made.

Reg wondered why the boomerang kept getting bigger until, all of a sudden, it hit him.

What should you take on a trip to the desert?

A thirst-aid kit!

Where can you find an ocean with no water?

On a map!

97

HEY!

A man arrived at a hotel where he had made a reservation rather late at night. All the lights were out, so he knocked on the door. After a long time a light appeared in an upstairs window and a woman called out, "Who are you? What do you want?" "I'm staying here!" the man replied. "Well, stay there, then," she shouted, and slammed the window shut.

What type of rocks are never found in the ocean?

Dry ones!

What did one campfire say to the other?

"Shall we go out tonight?"

RIDDLE

What can run but never walks, has a mouth but never talks, has a head but never weeps, has a bed but never sleeps?

A river!

Planes Trains & Unicycles

What do you get if you cross an Egyptian mummy with a car mechanic?

Toot and car man!

Customer: There's something wrong with my car. It has water in the carburettor.

Mechanic: Really? Water in the carburettor? I never heard of that before - I'll have to take a look at it. Where have you parked?

Customer: Er, in the lake!

HEY!

Which famous brothers didn't invent the aeroplane?

The Wrong brothers!

What did the jack say to the broken-down car?

"Can I give you a lift?"

What kind of vehicle needs a scare?

A hiccup truck!

hiccup!
hiccup!

What does a snail do on the motorway?

About 50cm an hour!

What do you call a very polite person who builds bridges and lays roads?

A civil engineer!

How did ancient Egyptians travel?

By Pharaoh-plane!

An old lady is driving carefully along the motorway, when a police car behind her indicates that she should pull over. "What have I done wrong?" she wonders. "I'm not speeding, I've got my seat belt on and all my documents are in order." The lady stops and lowers the window to speak to the officer, pointing to her ear and shaking her head to show that she can't hear very well. The policeman smiles and shouts, "I know! I'm here to tell you that your horn is stuck!"

FOR SALE SIGN!

You will need: An A4 piece of paper.

This is a great prank to pull on your parents and is so simple to do. Prepare a 'For Sale' sign to put in the window of their car, with a cheap price and a fake telephone number.

When you know your parents will be leaving the car for a few hours, stick the sign on one of the windows and wait for them to return. They will freak out at someone trying to sell their car, especially for such a low price!

PRANK LIKE A PRO: You could prepare the For Sale sign on a computer to disguise your handwriting. Don't forget to delete the file afterwards, though!

What do you call a dinosaur that's crashed his car?

Tyrannosaurus Wrecks!

What do you call a pretend railway?

A play station!

Why wasn't your father pleased when he bumped into an old friend?

They were both driving at the time!

Air Traffic Controller: what's your height and position, please?

Pilot: Well, I'm 6 foot tall and I'm sitting front left!

ROY'S DRIVING SCHOOL

LEARN TO DRIVE QUICKLY!
CRASH COURSES AVAILABLE

How do you catch a train?

You follow its tracks!

What did the dinosaur say after the car crash?

"I'm-so-saurus!"

What do you call a giant in an aeroplane seat?

Stuck!

MY

"It took me ages to work out how to fasten the seat belt in my son's new car, then all of a sudden it clicked!"

How does Jack Frost travel?

By icicle!

How can birds see what's behind them?

They look in their wing mirrors!

Why did the break dancer buy a car?

He fancied going for a spin!

If an electric train travels south, which way would the smoke go?

There wouldn't be any, it's an electric train!

Why did the farmer ride his horse to town?

It was too heavy to carry!

Which is the cleverest vehicle?

A Smart car!

An old gentleman was taking his first aeroplane trip. The stewardess handed him a piece of chewing gum. "It's to keep your ears from popping at high altitudes," she explained. When the plane landed the man rushed up to her. "Excuse me, miss," he said. "How do I get the gum out of my ears?"

MY ARM!

This is your pilot speaking - welcome aboard. We are pleased to have some of the best flight attendants in the industry... It's a pity none of them are on this flight!

What did the scuba diver say to the ship?

"I can see your bottom!"

What should you do with an old bike?

Recycle it.

RIDDLE

A cowboy rode to the Wild West Saloon on Friday. He stayed four nights and he left on Friday. How is this possible?

His horse was called Friday!

Goofy Gadgets

Why was the fly afraid of using the computer?

It didn't want to get tangled up in the web!

RIDDLE

What do you get after it has been taken?

¡A photo!

Hello, Grandpa!

MY ARM!

MOUSE TRAPPED!

You will need: A laser computer mouse.

While your victim is out, turn their computer mouse upside down and place a small piece of sticky tape over the laser.

When your victim tries to use the computer, they'll go crazy trying to figure out why it's not responding to their commands! It will take them a while to turn over the mouse and spot the prank!

PRANK LIKE A PRO: To make the prank even funnier, write 'Gotcha!' on a sticky note and use this to cover the laser instead of the tape. Your victim won't fail to see the funny side!

Sam: What type of ink do we use with this printer? Black, colour or iced?

Kyle: Iced ink?

Sam: Well, now you mention it, you do a bit!

What did the computer die of?

It had a terminal illness!

How does a barber save money on his phone calls?

He cuts them short!

BROKEN WINDOWS
Watch out for glass fragments!

What did the computer do at lunchtime?

It had a byte!

Customer: My computer doesn't work. The hard drive has crashed! What should I do?

IT Technician: Did you back up?

Customer, jumping out of his chair: Why? Is it going to explode?

What is the cheapest time to call your friends long distance?

When they're not home!

They told me to scan my laptop for viruses!

Alice: If you spend any more time working on that laptop, your back problem will get worse.

Lily: How do you know?

Alice: I'm not sure, it's just a hunch.

What do you get if you cross a telephone with an iron?

A smooth operator!

Did you hear about the monkey that left bits of food all over the computer?

His dad went bananas!

What do computer operators like to eat?

Chips!

Why was the thirsty alien hanging around the computer?

He was looking for the space bar!

What did the television order from the takeaway?

A satellite dish!

Where can you find Spider-man's home page?

On the world wide web!

Why do beavers spend a fortune on the internet?

They never want to log off!

Did you hear about the two aerials that got married?

They had a great reception!

What did Cinderella say when her photos didn't show up?

"Some day my prints will come!"

How does a dog stop a DVD player?

He presses the paws button!

I switched to Apple because every time I used Windows I wanted to fly into the monitor!

Medical Madness

What is as light as a feather, but you can't hold it for more than a few minutes, not even if you were the strongest man on earth?

Your breath!

"Doctor, doctor, I've swallowed a clock."
"Well, there's no cause for alarm!"

"Doctor, doctor, I smell like a fish."

"Oh, you poor sole!"

Doctor: Nurse, how is the little girl who swallowed a £1 coin last night?

Nurse: No change yet!

"Doctor, doctor, I've only got fifty seconds to live."

"Hang on. I'll be with you in a minute!"

"Doctor, doctor, I feel like a wasp."

"Buzz off! Can't you see I'm busy?"

THE BIG ITCH!

You will need: An old toothbrush and a T-shirt belonging to your victim.

Cut the soft bristles of an old toothbrush into tiny pieces.

Take a T-shirt from your victim's drawer and turn it inside out. Sprinkle a few bristles on the inside of the T-shirt and place it back where you found it.

When your victim gets dressed they'll start complaining about a terrible itch they have!

PRANK LIKE A PRO: Make sure you don't actually press the bristles into the material. For added drama, you could start scratching as well, pretending to have the same 'allergy'.

"Doctor, doctor, everybody thinks I'm a liar."

"Oh, come on. I find that hard to believe!"

"Doctor, doctor, I have purple spots at the back of my throat."

"OK. Go next door and stick out your tongue."

"Will that help?"

"No, but I can't stand the other doctor!"

Prisoner: Look here, doctor! You've already removed my spleen, tonsils, adenoids and one of my kidneys. I only came to see if you could get me out of this place!

Doctor: I am, bit by bit!

A man tells the doctor that his wife is going deaf. "Stand a little way from her and ask her a question," the doctor suggests. "If she doesn't answer, move closer and ask again. Keep going and you'll know how hard of hearing she really is." The man goes home and asks, "Honey, what's for dinner?" He doesn't hear an answer, so he moves closer and repeats the question several times until he's next to her. Finally, she answers. "For the eleventh time, I said we're having STEW!"

"Doctor, doctor, I feel like a piano."

"Sit down while I make some notes!"

What do you call a dentist who doesn't like tea?

Denis!

"Doctor, doctor, I've got strawberries growing out of my elbow."

"Oh, I've got some cream for that!"

Doctor, what does the X-ray of my head show?

Absolutely nothing!

Doctor: Nurse, did you take the patient's temperature?

Nurse: No. Is it missing?

"Doctor, doctor, I feel like an apple."

"We must get to the core of this!"

Looks like your athlete's foot has returned!

Patient: Doctor, do you have a cure for sleep walking?

Doctor: Sure, sprinkle drawing pins around your bed!

"Doctor, doctor, I keep on getting shooting pains in my eyes when I drink tea."

"Have you tried taking the spoon out?"

What did the banana go to the doctor?

Because it wasn't peeling well!

Patient: Doctor, I think I've swallowed a pillow.

Doctor: What do you feel?

Patient: A little down in the mouth!

"Doctor, doctor, I think I'm invisible."

"I'm sorry, I can't see you now!"

What do you call a dentist's office?

A filling station!

RIDDLE

What goes up and down but doesn't move?

Your temperature!

Patient: Doctor, I have yellow teeth. What do I do?

Dentist: Wear a brown tie!

"Doctor, doctor, I feel like a dog."

"Sit!"

Patient: How much will it cost to have this tooth taken out?

Dentist: £100.

Patient: Really?! £100 for just a few minutes work?

Dentist: Well, I can extract it very slowly if you like!

"Doctor, doctor, you've got to help me out."

"Certainly. Which way did you come in?"

What do you call an old dentist?

Long in the tooth!

Why did the prince go to the dentist?

To get crowned!

Did you hear about the judge who went to the dentist?

He asked him to extract the tooth, the whole tooth and nothing but the tooth!

What does a dentist do on a roller coaster?

He braces himself!

Monstrously Funny

When do ghosts normally appear?

Just before someone screams!

What is Dracula's favourite hot drink?

Decoffinated coffee!

Why did the one-eyed monster have to close his school?

He only had one pupil!

Why did the ghost starch her sheet?

So she could scare everyone stiff!

Which hairstyle do monsters like?

Deadlocks!

Who works in a monster hospital?

Skeleton staff!

What do you call two witches that live together?

Broommates!

What do you call a skeleton snake?

A rattler!

Urgh, there's a hair in my stew!

Who did the ghost invite to his party?

Anyone he could dig up!

What type of art do skeletons like?

Skulltures!

What did the daddy ghost say to his family when driving?

"Fasten your sheet belt!"

What do you call a ghostly bear?

Winnie the Oooooooooo!

What do you call a motorbike that belongs to a witch?

A brrrooooommmm stick!

Why can't skeletons play music in church?

Because they have no organs!

What did one witch say to the other witch when she was asked for a lift?

"There's always broom for one more!"

What did the ghost teacher say to his class?

"Watch the board and I'll go through it again!"

Why did the twin witches wear name tags?

So you could tell which witch was which!

What does the metal monster want written on his gravestone?

Rust in Peace!

You don't fool me! I can see right through you!

How do ghosts make milkshake?

They sneak up behind a cow and yell 'Boo!'

Why was the Egyptian boy upset?

His daddy was a mummy!

Why did the vampire's wife complain so much?

Her husband was a pain in the neck!

During which age did mummies live?

The band-age!

Where do ghosts go on holiday?

Death Valley!

How many zombies make a stink?

A phew!

What do short-sighted ghosts wear?

Spooktacles!

What do you do if you see a skeleton running across the road?

Jump out of your skin and join him!

How did the doctor bring the ghost back to life?

He took it to the living room!

Why did the mummy have no friends?

He was too wrapped up in himself!

Why are skeletons so calm?

Because nothing gets under their skin!

What do little ghosts drink?

Evaporated milk!

Why is the letter V like a monster?

It comes after U!

What does a monster mummy say to her children at lunch?

"Don't speak with someone in your mouth!"

HAUNTED ROOM!

You will need: A bathroom with a mirror and a shower, a cotton wool ball and a small bowl of lemon juice.

Dip the cotton wool ball into the bowl and squeeze out the excess juice so that it won't drip.

With the wet cotton wool write a short, scary message on the mirror. You could write 'THIS ROOM IS HAUNTED' or simply 'BOO!'

Let the juice dry and wait until someone takes a shower. When the room steams up, the ghostly message will appear. A scream will follow shortly afterwards!

PRANK LIKE A PRO: Make sure the juice is really dry on the mirror. To check the effect, breathe on the letters to see them appear as if by magic.

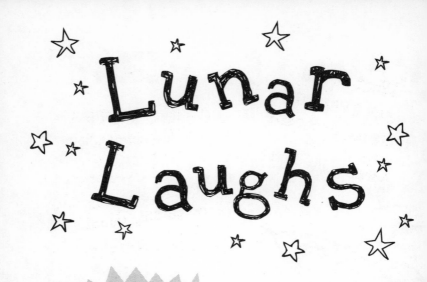

Lunar Laughs

Why do astronauts like subtractions?

They are always ready to countdown!

What's the main use for flying saucers?

To hold flying cups!

RIDDLE

I only work when I am fired. What am I?

A rocket!

What do you call a wizard from outer space?

A flying sorcerer!

Why did the boy become an astronaut?

Because he was no earthly good!

Two astronauts were in a spaceship circling high above the Earth. One had to go on a spacewalk while the other stayed inside. When the spacewalker tried to get back inside the spaceship, he discovered that the cabin door was locked, so he knocked. There was no answer. He knocked again, louder this time. There was still no answer. Finally he hammered at the door as hard as he could and heard a voice from inside the spaceship saying, "Who's there?"

What do you do if you see a spaceman?

Park in it, man!

What did the alien say when he was out of room?

I'm all spaced out!

Why don't astronauts get on well with other people?

They are not always down-to-earth!

What do aliens do when they're bored?

Play astronauts and crosses!

What did the astronaut see on the stove?

An identified frying object!

What did E.T.'s parents ask him when he got home?

"Where on Earth have you been?"

Why do aliens make crop circles?

Because they are corny!

Why did Mickey Mouse go to space?

To visit Pluto!

How do you send a baby astronaut to sleep?

You rock-et!

What type of poetry do astronauts write in space?

Uni-verses!

space poems

OOPS!

What does an astronaut do when he gets angry?

He blasts off!

How do you ask directions in space?

Ask-eroid!

Living on Earth is expensive, but you do get a free trip around the Sun every year!

What goes in one year and out the other?

A time machine!

How do you know that the moon and the earth are good friends?

They have been going around together for years!

How many astronomers does it take to change a light bulb?

None - astronomers aren't afraid of the dark!

What holds the moon up?

Moon beams!

Why don't astronauts keep their jobs very long?

Because as soon as they start, they get fired!

Did you hear about the cow astronaut?

He landed on the moooooon!

What do you get if you cross a student with an alien?

Something from another universe-ity!

What do you call an alien spaceship that drips water?

A crying saucer!

Why are astronauts successful people?

Because they always go up in the world!

What do you call a loony spaceman?

An astro-nut!

Full!

What do astronauts wear to keep warm?

Apollo neck jumpers!

Why didn't the astronauts stay on the moon?

Because it was a full moon and there was no room!

What do astronauts put on their toast?

Space jam!

OOPS!

What do you get if you cross an alien and a hot drink?

Gravi-tea!

Can you name an astronaut's favourite game?

Moon-opoly!

Last night, as I laid in bed looking at the stars, I thought to myself... 'Where's the ceiling?!'